INSPIRATION

FOR

MUSICIANS

EMILY DARCY

summersdale

INSPIRATION FOR MUSICIANS

Summersdale Publishers Ltd
46 West Street
Chichester
West Sussex
PO19 1RP
UK

www.summersdale.com

Printed and bound in the Czech Republic

ISBN: 978-1-78685-058-4

Substantial discounts on bulk quantities of Summersdale books are available to corporations, professional associations and other organisations. For details contact general enquiries: telephone: +44 (0) 1243 771107, fax: +44 (0) 1243 786300 or email: enquiries@summersdale.com.

To.....................................

From.................................

I can only think of
music as something
inherent in every
human being –
a birthright. Music
coordinates mind,
body and spirit.

Yehudi Menuhin

WITHOUT MUSIC, LIFE WOULD BE A MISTAKE.

Friedrich Nietzsche

Music doesn't lie. If there is something to be changed in this world, then it can only happen through music.

Jimi Hendrix

Sounds like the blues
are composed of feeling,
finesse and fear.

Billy Gibbons

MUSIC IS THE SPACE BETWEEN THE NOTES.

Claude Debussy

First you master
your instrument,
then you master
the music; then you
forget about all that...
and just play.

Charlie Parker

A bird does not sing
because he has an answer.
He sings because
he has a song.

Joan Walsh Anglund

MUSIC IS AN OUTBURST OF THE SOUL.

Frederick Delius

All deep things
are Song. It seems
somehow the very
central essence of
us, Song; as if all
the rest were but
wrappages and hulls!

Thomas Carlyle

A SYMPHONY MUST BE LIKE THE WORLD. IT MUST EMBRACE EVERYTHING.

Gustav Mahler

I've never known a musician
who regretted being one.

Virgil Thomson

Bach opens a vista to the universe. After experiencing him, people feel there is meaning to life after all.

Helmut Walcha

MUSIC, WHEN SOFT VOICES DIE, VIBRATES IN THE MEMORY.

Percy Bysshe Shelley

I know that the most joy in my life has come to me **from my violin.**

Albert Einstein

A great song should destroy cop cars and set fire to the suburbs. I'm only interested in writing great songs.

Tom Morello

SING LUSTILY AND WITH A GOOD COURAGE... LIFT UP YOUR VOICE WITH STRENGTH.

John Wesley

I have always believed that opera is a planet where the muses work together, join hands and celebrate all the arts.

Franco Zeffirelli

IN THE PATTERNS OF MUSIC AND ALL THE ARTS ARE THE KEYS OF LEARNING.

Plato

Alas for those that never sing,
But die with all their
music in them!

Oliver Wendell Holmes Sr

Rock's so good to me.
Rock is my child and
my grandfather.

Chuck Berry

LEARNING MUSIC BY READING ABOUT IT IS LIKE MAKING LOVE BY MAIL.

Luciano Pavarotti

The piano is able to communicate the subtlest universal truths by means of **wood, metal and vibrating air.**

Kenneth Miller

Virtue is the strong
stem of man's nature,
and music is the
blossoming of virtue.

Confucius

I SING LIKE I FEEL.

Ella Fitzgerald

My heart, which is so
full to overflowing,
has often been
solaced and refreshed
by music when
sick and weary.

Martin Luther

GUITAR PLAYING IS A RELEASE, LIBERATION. PUT SIMPLY, IT IS FREEDOM.

W. C. Handy

Music is the shorthand
of emotion.

Leo Tolstoy

I play every gig as if it could be my last, then I enjoy it more than ever.

Nigel Kennedy

YOU ARE THE MUSIC WHILE THE MUSIC LASTS.

T. S. Eliot

In order to compose, all you need to do is remember a tune that **nobody else has thought of.**

Robert Schumann

To stop the flow of music would be like the stopping of time itself, incredible and inconceivable.

Aaron Copland

DON'T PLAY WHAT'S THERE. PLAY WHAT'S NOT THERE.

Miles Davis

It's easy to play any
musical instrument:
all you have to do
is touch the right
key at the right time
and the instrument
will play itself.

Johann Sebastian Bach

MUSIC IS THE LANGUAGE SPOKEN BY THE ANGELS.

Naphtali Herz Imber

Music expresses that which
cannot be said and on which
it is impossible to be silent.

Victor Hugo

What have I got?
No looks, no money,
no education. Just talent.

Sammy Davis Jr

THERE IS NO
FEELING, PERHAPS,
EXCEPT THE
EXTREMES OF FEAR
AND GRIEF, THAT
DOES NOT FIND
RELIEF IN MUSIC.

George Eliot

Seemed to me that drumming was the best way to get **close to God.**

Lionel Hampton

The music soars within
the little lark,
And the lark soars.

Elizabeth Barrett Browning

ROCK 'N' ROLL: MUSIC FOR THE NECK DOWNWARDS.

Keith Richards

I think music in itself
is healing. It's an
explosive expression
of humanity. It's
something we are
all touched by.

Billy Joel

WHAT PASSION CANNOT MUSIC RAISE AND QUELL?

John Dryden

I'm an interpreter of stories.
When I perform it's like I'm
just sitting down at my piano
and telling fairy stories.

Nat King Cole

After silence, that which comes nearest to expressing the inexpressible is music.

Aldous Huxley

GOOD MUSIC STIRS
BY ITS MYSTERIOUS
RESEMBLANCE TO
THE OBJECTS AND
FEELINGS WHICH
MOTIVATED IT.

Jean Cocteau

Do you not know
that our soul is
**composed of
harmony?**

Leonardo da Vinci

We are the music makers,
And we are the
dreamers of dreams.

Arthur O'Shaughnessy

MUSIC CAN CHANGE THE WORLD BECAUSE IT CAN CHANGE PEOPLE.

Bono

If I were to begin
life again, I would
devote it to music.
It is the only cheap
and unpunished
rapture upon earth.

Sydney Smith

MUSIC WASHES AWAY FROM THE SOUL THE DUST OF EVERYDAY LIFE.

Berthold Auerbach

Music, even in situations
of the greatest horror,
should never be painful to
the ear but should flatter
and charm it, and thereby
always remain music.

Wolfgang Amadeus Mozart

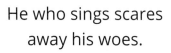

He who sings scares
away his woes.

Miguel de Cervantes

RHYTHM AND HARMONY FIND THEIR WAY INTO THE INWARD PLACES OF THE SOUL.

Plato

Music is enough
for a lifetime – but
a lifetime is **not
enough for music**.

Sergei Rachmaninoff

Truly there would be reason to go mad were it not for music.

Pyotr Ilyich Tchaikovsky

MUSIC IS
WHAT LIFE
SOUNDS
═ LIKE. ═

Eric Olson

Great art is as
irrational as great
music. It is mad with
its own loveliness.

George Jean Nathan

WHERE WORDS FAIL, MUSIC SPEAKS.

Hans Christian Andersen

Music is the voice that tells
us that the human race is
greater than it knows.

Napoleon Bonaparte

The best music [is]
essentially there to
provide you something
to face the world with.

Bruce Springsteen

I HAVE NO PLEASURE
IN ANY MAN WHO
DESPISES MUSIC. IT
IS NO INVENTION
OF OURS: IT IS A
GIFT OF GOD.

Martin Luther

I am in the world only for the **purpose of composing.**

Franz Schubert

I did think I did see all Heaven before me, and the great God himself.

George Frideric Handel

COUNTRY MUSIC IS THREE CHORDS AND THE TRUTH.

Harlan Howard

Music is the art
which is most nigh to
tears and memory.

Oscar Wilde

MUSIC HELPS YOU FIND THE TRUTHS YOU MUST BRING INTO THE REST OF YOUR LIFE.

Alanis Morissette

Such sweet compulsion
doth in music lie.

John Milton

To send light into
the darkness of men's
hearts – such is the
duty of the artist.

Robert Schumann

TAKE A MUSIC-BATH
ONCE OR TWICE A
WEEK FOR A FEW
SEASONS, AND YOU
WILL FIND THAT IT IS
TO THE SOUL WHAT
THE WATER-BATH
IS TO THE BODY.

Oliver Wendell Holmes Sr

Music produces a kind of pleasure which human nature **cannot do without.**

Confucius

If music be the food
of love, play on;
Give me excess of it.

William Shakespeare

WHAT WE PLAY

═IS LIFE.═

Louis Armstrong

A musician's or artist's responsibility is a simple one, and that is, through your music to tell the truth.

Tom Morello

MAKE MUSIC AND WORK AT IT.

Plato

Even the smallest task
in music is so absorbing,
and carries us so far away
from town, country, earth,
and all worldly things.

Felix Mendelssohn

Music, once admitted to the soul, becomes a sort of spirit, and never dies.

Edward Bulwer-Lytton

MUSIC IS NOTHING ELSE BUT WILD SOUNDS CIVILISED INTO TIME AND TUNE.

Thomas Fuller

If you look deep enough you will see music; the heart of nature being **everywhere music.**

Thomas Carlyle

A jazz musician is a juggler who uses harmonies instead of oranges.

Benny Green

MUSIC
CAN BRING
A TEAR TO
—≡— YOUR EYE. —≡—

Harold Wheeler

Technically, I'm
not even a guitar
player; all I play is
truth and emotion.

Jimi Hendrix

WHEN WORDS LEAVE OFF, MUSIC BEGINS.

Heinrich Heine

Let me have music dying,
and I seek
No more delight.

John Keats

The blues tells a story.
Every line of the blues
has a meaning.

John Lee Hooker

MUSIC IS THE LANGUAGE OF THE SPIRIT. IT OPENS THE SECRET OF LIFE, BRINGING PEACE, ABOLISHING STRIFE.

Kahlil Gibran

I pay no attention
whatever to anybody's
praise or blame.
I simply follow my
own feelings.

Wolfgang Amadeus Mozart

If I were not a physicist,
I would probably be
a musician... I see my
life in terms of music.

Albert Einstein

WHO HEARS MUSIC FEELS HIS SOLITUDE PEOPLED AT ONCE.

Robert Browning

If a composer could
say what he had to
say in words he would
not bother trying
to say it in music.

Gustav Mahler

JAZZ IS NOT DEAD – IT JUST SMELLS FUNNY.

Frank Zappa

If a man were permitted
to make all the ballads he
need not care who should
make the laws of a nation.

Andrew Fletcher

Music is indeed
the mediator between
the spiritual and the
sensual life.

Ludwig van Beethoven

THE HISTORY OF A PEOPLE IS FOUND IN ITS SONGS.

George Jellinek

A painter paints his pictures on canvas. But musicians paint their **pictures on silence.**

Leopold Stokowski

If you can walk
you can dance.
If you can talk
you can sing.

Zimbabwean proverb

WORKS OF ART MAKE RULES; RULES DON'T MAKE WORKS OF ART.

Claude Debussy

There is no truer
truth obtainable
By Man than
comes of music.

Robert Browning

MOURNFUL AND YET GRAND IS THE DESTINY OF THE ARTIST.

Franz Liszt

Music was my refuge. I
could crawl into the space
between the notes and curl
my back to loneliness.

Maya Angelou

I haven't understood a
bar of music in my life
but I have felt it.

Igor Stravinsky

WITHOUT CRAFTSMANSHIP, INSPIRATION IS A MERE REED SHAKEN IN THE WIND.

Johannes Brahms

There was no one
near to confuse me
so I was forced to
become original.

Joseph Haydn

The musician is perhaps
the most modest of
animals, but he is
also the proudest.

Erik Satie

MUSIC MELTS ALL THE SEPARATE PARTS OF OUR BODIES TOGETHER.

Anaïs Nin

A creative artist works on his next composition because he is not satisfied with his previous one.

Dmitri Shostakovich

THE CITY IS BUILT TO MUSIC.

Alfred, Lord Tennyson

Inspiration is an awakening,
a quickening of all man's
faculties and it is manifested in
all high artistic achievements.

Giacomo Puccini

Music is the art of the prophets, the only art that calms the agitations of the soul.

Martin Luther

THE ONLY LOVE AFFAIR I EVER HAD WAS WITH MUSIC.

Maurice Ravel

The beautiful thing
about learning is that
**nobody can take it
away from you.**

B. B. King

Music is a higher
revelation than all
wisdom and philosophy.

Ludwig van Beethoven

LEARNING NEVER EXHAUSTS THE MIND.

Leonardo da Vinci

Motivation gets you
going and habit
gets you there.

Zig Ziglar

MUSIC IS THE POETRY OF THE AIR.

Jean Paul

I often think in music. I live
my daydreams in music.

Albert Einstein

Music is your own
experience, your own
thoughts, your wisdom.

Charlie Parker

I CALL ARCHITECTURE FROZEN MUSIC.

Johann Wolfgang
von Goethe

Music is forever;
music should grow
and mature with you,
following you right
on up **until you die.**

Paul Simon

Music, being identical with heaven, isn't a thing of momentary thrills, or even hourly ones. It's a condition of eternity.

Gustav Holst

THE TRUEST EXPRESSION OF A PEOPLE IS IN ITS DANCE AND MUSIC.

Agnes de Mille

It's something we
are all touched by.
No matter what
culture you're from,
everyone loves music.

Billy Joel

IN MUSIC THE
PASSIONS
ENJOY
THEMSELVES.

Friedrich Nietzsche

Music can change the world.

Ludwig van Beethoven

Music, the greatest good that mortals know, and all of heaven we have below.

Joseph Addison

ALL THAT COUNTS IN LIFE IS INTENTION.

Andrea Bocelli

We do not play the piano with our fingers but **with our mind.**

Glenn Gould

Those who have achieved
all their aims probably
set them too low.

Herbert von Karajan

THE WORD 'LISTEN' CONTAINS THE SAME LETTERS AS THE WORD 'SILENT'.

Alfred Brendel

Every great work of
art has two faces,
one toward its
own time and one
toward the future,
toward eternity.

Daniel Barenboim

PLAYING LIFTS YOU OUT OF YOURSELF INTO A DELIRIOUS PLACE.

Jacqueline du Pré

When you play, never
mind who listens to you.

Robert Schumann

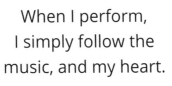

When I perform,
I simply follow the
music, and my heart.

Lang Lang

THE CHALLENGE IS
NOT SO MUCH TO
CHANGE THE SOUND.
THE CHALLENGE
IS TO CONNECT
AND TO CREATE
SOMETHING SPECIAL.

Gustavo Dudamel

Music is the divine way to tell beautiful, poetic things to the **heart.**

Pablo Casals

Setting my mind on
a musical instrument
was like falling in love.
All the world seemed
bright and changed.

W. C. Handy

MUSIC IS EVERYBODY'S POSSESSION.

John Lennon

Music is a friend of labour for it lightens the task by refreshing the nerves and spirit of the worker.

William Green

EVERYTHING IN THE UNIVERSE HAS A RHYTHM, EVERYTHING DANCES.

Maya Angelou

The only truth is music.

Jack Kerouac

If you cannot teach me to fly, teach me to sing.

J. M. Barrie

MUSIC BRINGS A
WARM GLOW TO MY
VISION, THAWING
THE MIND AND
MUSCLE FROM
THEIR ENDLESS
WINTERING.

Haruki Murakami

Music is moonlight
in the gloomy
night of life.

Jean Paul

Music is the universal language of mankind.

Henry Wadsworth Longfellow

LIFE IS ONE GRAND, SWEET SONG, SO START THE MUSIC.

Ronald Reagan

Are we not formed,
as notes of music are,
For one another,
though dissimilar?

Percy Bysshe Shelley

IMAGINATION CREATES REALITY.

Richard Wagner

Music is all around us;
the world is full of it,
and you simply take as
much as you require.

Edward Elgar

Music can name
the unnameable
and communicate
the unknowable.

Leonard Bernstein

WITHOUT MUSIC, LIFE WOULD BE A BLANK TO ME.

Jane Austen

There's nothing like the eureka moment of knocking off a song that **didn't exist before.**

Paul McCartney

Silence is the fabric
upon which the
notes are woven.

Lawrence Duncan

THE PAUSE IS AS IMPORTANT AS THE NOTE.

Truman Fisher

It is incontestable
that music induces
in us a sense of
the infinite and
the contemplation
of the invisible.

Victor de Laprade

MUSIC IS WELL SAID TO BE THE SPEECH OF ANGELS.

Thomas Carlyle

Truly to sing, that is a
different breath.

Rainer Maria Rilke

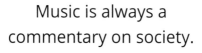

Music is always a
commentary on society.

Frank Zappa

If you're interested in finding out more about our books, find us on Facebook at Summersdale Publishers and follow us on Twitter at @Summersdale.

www.summersdale.com